I0797360

CORPORATE ★ AMERICA

Airbnb

Blaine Wiseman

LIGHTBOX
openlightbox.com

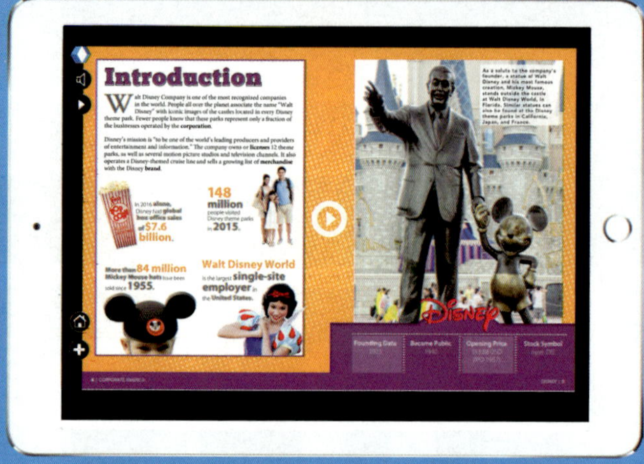

Lightbox is an all-inclusive digital solution for the teaching and learning of curriculum topics in an original, groundbreaking way. Lightbox is based on National Curriculum Standards.

STANDARD FEATURES OF LIGHTBOX

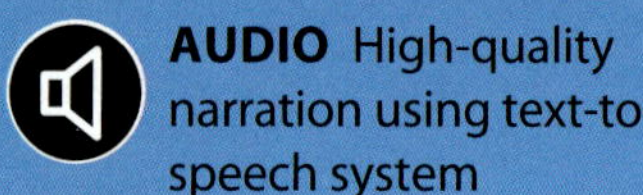

AUDIO High-quality narration using text-to-speech system

ACTIVITIES Printable PDFs that can be emailed and graded

SLIDESHOWS Pictorial overviews of key concepts

VIDEOS Embedded high-definition video clips

WEBLINKS Curated links to external, child-safe resources

TRANSPARENCIES Step-by-step layering of maps, diagrams, charts, and timelines

INTERACTIVE MAPS Interactive maps and aerial satellite imagery

QUIZZES Ten multiple choice questions that are automatically graded and emailed for teacher assessment

KEY WORDS Matching key concepts to their definitions

Contents

Introduction

Every **corporation** is built by people. A corporation represents and serves the business interests of the people who operate it. In doing so, it provides products or services to consumers. Airbnb provides a service that connects vendors, who have accommodations to rent, with consumers looking for a place to stay.

Airbnb began as a **start-up**, growing from a simple idea to a billion-dollar corporation in only a few years. Today, it serves as a digital marketplace, providing a platform on which property owners can rent their homes to guests. Its revolutionary approach to accommodations has changed the hospitality and tourism industry all over the world.

Airbnb properties are available in **191 countries** around the world.

More than **200 million guests** have stayed in properties listed on **Airbnb**.

On any given night, there will be approximately **2 million people** staying in other people's homes **thanks to Airbnb**.

Airbnb's **#1 market** is **Paris, France**. It has more than **78,000 listed properties**.

In 2016, Airbnb partnered with the Aquarium Paris in France, holding a contest that allowed the winners to spend a night in an underwater room with the facility's sharks. The promotion helped teach people more about sharks while also showcasing the variety of accommodations offered by Airbnb.

Founding Date	Ownership	Estimated Value	Area Served
2008	Private	$31 billion	Global

Beginnings

Airbnb grew out of a simple idea. When a large conference was scheduled in San Francisco in 2007, Joe Gebbia and Brian Chesky saw an opportunity. The roommates realized that some people attending the conference may not want to pay high prices for a hotel room. As an alternative, the two men offered a place to sleep in their apartment. They put their skills in **entrepreneurship** and design to work, and built a website. Since they did not have an extra bed, they put an air mattress on the floor, offering an airbed and breakfast for their guests. The airbedandbreakfast.com website attracted far more people than expected.

Gebbia and Chesky realized there was a large, untapped market for these types of accommodations. They hired a friend, Nathan Blecharczyk, to develop the website for them, and began working to expand the business. In need of money, the men launched a fundraising project at the Democratic National Convention in Denver, Colorado. They put together custom cereal boxes featuring the two major figures in that year's federal election and sold them for $40 each. By the end of the convention, 800 boxes of Obama O's and Cap'n McCain's had been sold, raising more than $30,000. Following the success of their marketing scheme, the founders were invited to attend a training program at Y-Combinator, a start-up **incubator** in California's Silicon Valley.

New York City is America's most popular tourist destination, attracting more than 50 million visitors every year.

While at Y-Combinator, the founders realized that they could be more successful if they built stronger relationships with their hosts. They decided to focus on their properties in New York City first. The men traveled to the city to meet with people who had listed properties on the company's website. They took pictures and wrote reviews of the properties, and placed them on the website. The men also shortened the company name from Air Bed and Breakfast to Airbnb. A month later, Airbnb was able to secure more than $600,000 in funding from **investors**, allowing the founders to actively begin building their business.

Airbnb was never meant to be the big idea. It was meant to be the thing that paid the rent so we could think of the big idea.
– Brian Chesky, Airbnb Co-founder and **Chief Executive Officer (CEO)**

Corporate Timeline

Airbnb is sometimes seen as an overnight success. However, growing Airbnb from an airbed on the floor of an apartment to a large corporation did not happen immediately. The company has overcome many logistical and technological obstacles along the way.

2007

Room for Rent
Brian Chesky and Joe Gebbia create a website to rent an airbed on the floor of their San Francisco apartment.

2008

Adding a Founder
Chesky and Gebbia invite Nathan Blecharczyk to become their first engineer. He becomes a co-founder of the company, Air Bed and Breakfast.

2008

Marketing Politics
A marketing campaign launched at the Democratic National Convention earns the struggling entrepreneurs more than $30,000.

2009

A New Beginning
Air Bed and Breakfast joins Y-Combinator and changes its name to Airbnb.

2009

Investing Interest
A $600,000 **venture capital** investment signals a major turning point for Airbnb.

Big Money
Airbnb reaches a valuation of $30 billion.

Reaching New Heights
Airbnb reaches 1 million nights booked and a $1 billion **valuation**.

2011

2011

2014

2016

The Backup Plan After two hosts have their homes damaged by renters, Airbnb guarantees $50,000 to cover costs of damages for any host. This is later increased to $1 million.

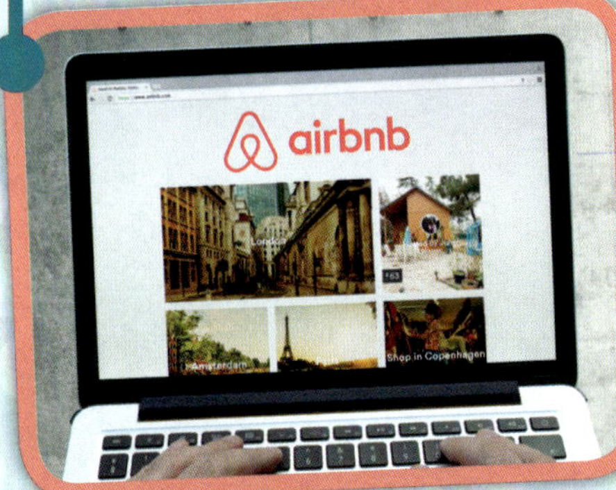

A New Look
Airbnb redesigns its website and **app**, and unveils a new **logo**.

Airbnb Today

Millions of people around the world use Airbnb to find accommodations for their travels. Millions of others use it to offer accommodations to travelers. This was the original premise and vision for the company. From this simple premise, Airbnb has grown into a leader in the hospitality industry.

Leadership has not come without challenges, however. Through the years, Airbnb has encountered resistance from other members of the hospitality industry. Airbnb's major competitors are established corporations such as hotel chains and tour operators. These competitors have suffered from Airbnb's success. Several have tried to slow Airbnb's progress and, in some cases, shut it down. Airbnb has pushed forward in spite of these roadblocks, continuing to expand its business into new areas.

Business travel is a major part of the global travel industry, and one in which Airbnb has worked hard to find success. In 2015, Airbnb created its Airbnb For Business division. The following year, it reached agreements with major corporate booking agents that would make it easier for business travelers to stay with Airbnb For Business. The company's website and app now feature a tool that can ensure homes and apartments are "Business Travel Ready." With these changes, Airbnb has increased its business use from 250 companies in 2015 to more than 250,000 today.

Besides hotel chains, Airbnb has also faced other challenges to its business model. In 2015, some New York residents protested that the company's rental properties were having a negative impact on their communities.

"We are thinking about the travel experience end-to-end. The real focus is doing something different."
– Nathan Blecharczyk,
Airbnb Co-founder and
Chief Strategy Officer

A World of Airbnb

Airbnb has a presence in almost every corner of the world. As the company has grown, it has set up teams of employees in key regions. Together, they manage the marketplace, offering more than 4 million houses, apartments, and other accommodations in diverse locations around the globe.

ARCTIC OCEAN

NORTH AMERICA

PACIFIC OCEAN

1

SOUTH AMERICA

ATLANTIC OCEAN

2

MAP LEGEND

- Featured Location
- Land
- Water

0 1,000 Miles
0 1,000 Kilometers

SOUTHERN OCEAN

ANTARCTICA

1 **Corporate Headquarters** Airbnb's main office is in its founding city of San Francisco. The office is located in a former warehouse space in the city's SoMa district. More than 1,200 employees work there.

2 **South American Regional Office** Airbnb's South American operations are based in São Paulo, Brazil. The office covers 3,875 square feet (360 square meters). Brazilian design accents can be found throughout the space.

3 **European Headquarters** Dublin, Ireland, is home to Airbnb's European headquarters. Opened in 2016, the office has 21,000 square feet (2,000 sq. m) of space. Its reception area has been modeled after an Irish pub.

4 **Chinese Operations** After struggling to find success in China, Airbnb changed its name in the country to *Aibiying*, which means "welcome each other with love." Its main office is located in the city of Beijing.

5 **Australian Headquarters** Airbnb's Australian operations are based in Sydney. The office's design pays tribute to Australian culture. Goalposts at the entrance, for instance, recognize the country's love of football.

Branding Airbnb

Airbnb has grown from an unknown start-up to a company that spans the world. The name Airbnb has now come to represent a new way of traveling. Its **branding** is targeted toward people who want a different type of travel experience. Airbnb promises its guests a unique experience and a real feeling of home away from home.

Sharing Airbnb's entire premise is based on the **sharing economy**. This concept is new to many people. The idea of staying in someone else's home, or having someone stay in their own home, can be unsettling. People worry about their personal and material safety. Airbnb promotes the sharing economy as a safe way to travel. It does this by focusing on how using its sharing-based services creates a sense of community and friendship among the participants. By confronting its guests' fears, Airbnb helps people feel at ease about the company and the services it offers.

Freedom What sets Airbnb apart from competitors is the diversity of accommodations and experiences it offers. Hotels, campgrounds, and other more traditional accommodation options can be limiting in terms of location, price, amenities, experiences, and comfort. The Airbnb website and app offers guests advanced search tools that can be used to access a wide range of properties, with a variety of pricing options and amenities. Guests are free to choose the property or experience that works best for them. This type of freedom is changing the way millions of people travel.

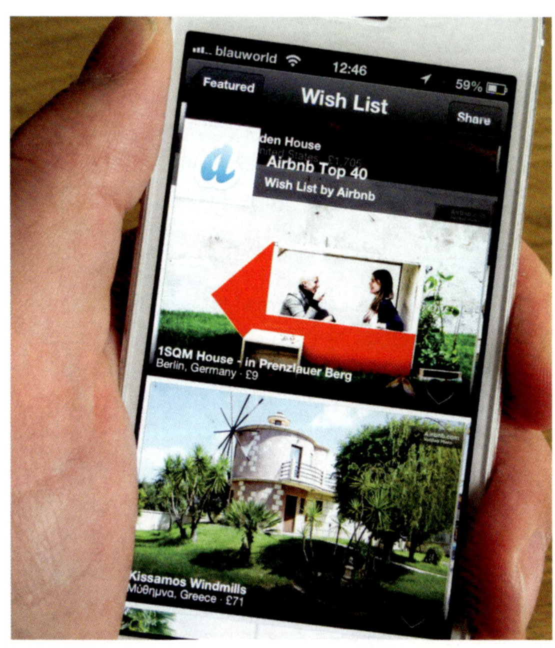

Adventure Taking the freedom of choice even further, Airbnb's diverse listings include unique offerings that users would not find anywhere else. If a traveler wants the royal treatment, he or she can choose to stay in one of Airbnb's castle properties. For complete privacy, Airbnb users can rent private islands. For those who want a natural setting, treehouses are available in a variety of locations. Private yachts can be rented and sailed, while houseboats can cruise lakes and canals. A clock tower in London, England, offers great views and a unique vantage point. Airbnb has become the preferred choice for accommodations for millions of adventurous travelers around the world.

Company Name

The company name, Airbnb Inc., was created as a way to describe the founders' first offering of accommodations. "Airb" represents the air mattress they provided as a bed for their guests, while "nb" indicates the breakfast that came with the arrangement.

Company Logo

Airbnb launched its current logo in 2014. Called the Bélo, it is a distinctive "A" design that is meant to evoke images of a person, a heart, a location pin, and the company name. Together, these images symbolize the company's ideals of togetherness and belonging.

Company Slogan

The company has used several **slogans** over the years. Slogans such as "Belong, Anywhere" promote the company's ideals. They put forward the idea that guests can go anywhere they want using Airbnb and experience a feeling of belonging when they get there.

The Art of Selling

Airbnb has found success in an industry that was previously dominated by traditional ideas and technologies. Although the company has now become a part of many people's lives, it was not an easy process. Selling consumers on the advantages of its services took time, patience, and expertise. While the company relies largely on word of mouth to attract users, it has also launched successful advertising campaigns to bring attention to its offerings.

Views Airbnb released its first global ad campaign in 2014. Called "Views," the campaign was run on digital and mobile platforms, as well as in theaters and on airliners. The campaign's commercial showed the views that guests could see from the windows of various hosts' homes. When viewed online, the ad linked to **microsites**, where viewers could search for listings in their own language. The goal of the campaign was to show travelers how enjoyable and inexpensive it can be to experience new places the same way the locals do.

Never a Stranger Airbnb's 2015 "Never a Stranger" campaign was created to address people's fears about staying in a stranger's home. The campaign's TV commercial featured a real Airbnb guest named Ellie writing a letter to her hosts. In the letter, she reminisces about the time she spent with them. She notes how comfortable and "at home" they made her feel. As she speaks, the viewer watches Ellie meeting new people and enjoying different locales. The message is that the world is just one big welcoming community waiting to be experienced through Airbnb.

Live There In 2016, Airbnb launched its "Live There" advertising campaign. It was the largest ad campaign in the company's history. Featuring 15-, 30-, and 60-second television commercials and ads in magazines and newspapers, the campaign urged travelers to do more than just visit a destination. Along with advertising, Airbnb also updated its app and website to include guidebooks. Using these books, guests can now obtain tips and information from people who live in specific places. They can also find local activities and attractions away from crowds of tourists. The idea is to help visitors feel like they "Live there. Even if it's just for a night."

Millennials, or people born between 1982 and 2004, account for roughly **60%** of **Airbnb bookings**.

Airbnb's **Live There videos** have ***more than*** **70 million views** online.

In 2015 alone, **Airbnb** spent more than **$23 million on advertising**.

Competitors

Airbnb competes with a variety of hospitality and tourism companies. Its accommodation services put it in direct competition with hotels. Many hotel chains have responded to this competition by adding new features to their services and special offers designed to attract customers away from Airbnb. Other competitors are more closely aligned to Airbnb, offering similar services and arrangements.

Marriott

STOCK SYMBOL nasdaq: MAR

Marriott International Inc. is the largest hotelier in the world. Through major acquisitions in 2015 and 2016, Marriott grew to control more than 5,700 hotels worldwide. These include hotel brands such as Delta, Westin, Sheraton, Ritz-Carlton, and Bulgari. With these acquisitions, Marriott is now the only hotel chain with a higher **market value** than that of Airbnb.

tripadvisor

STOCK SYMBOL nasdaq: TRIP

TripAdvisor is the world's largest online travel community. One of its main draws is that users can book everything they need for their trip through the TripAdvisor website. From accommodations to flights, rental cars, restaurants, and activities, TripAdvisor aggregates almost everything a traveler needs in one place. This practical and easy-to-use platform makes TripAdvisor popular with users around the world.

STOCK SYMBOL nasdaq: EXPE

Founded in 1996 by a division of the computer giant Microsoft, Expedia is an online travel booking site similar to TripAdvisor. Its website offers visitors the opportunity to plan everything from an overnight stay to an entire vacation. The company operates several brands, including Hotels.com and Travelocity. In 2015, it acquired HomeAway, a site that provides vacation rental listings. With this purchase, Expedia is now going head-to-head with Airbnb.

Comparison Chart

Businesses keep records to track their **assets**, **liabilities**, **profits**, and losses. Companies use this data to guide expansion and cost-cutting decisions. Investors use the information to help them decide where to invest their money. They will also refer to a company's **market capitalization** or market valuation to gauge public confidence in the business.

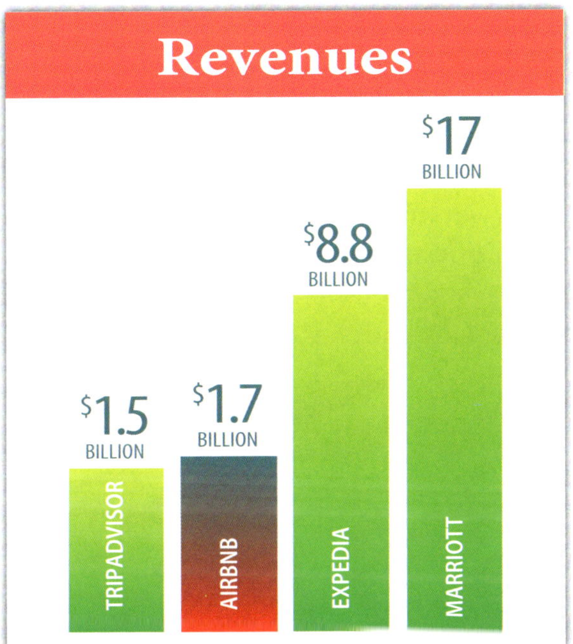

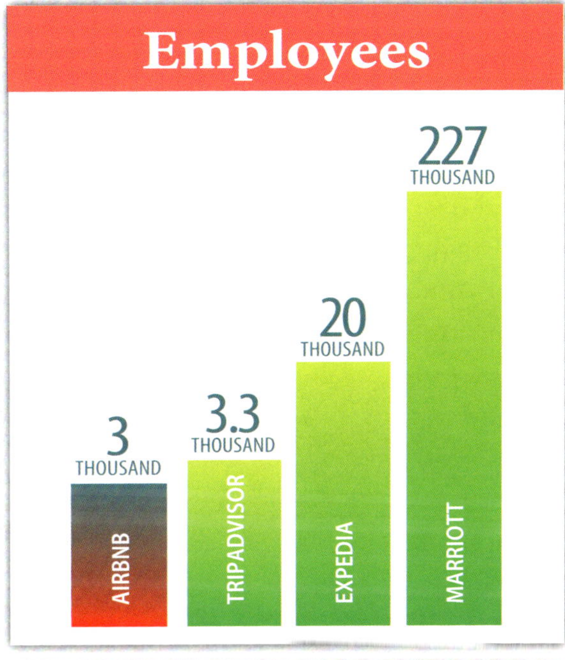

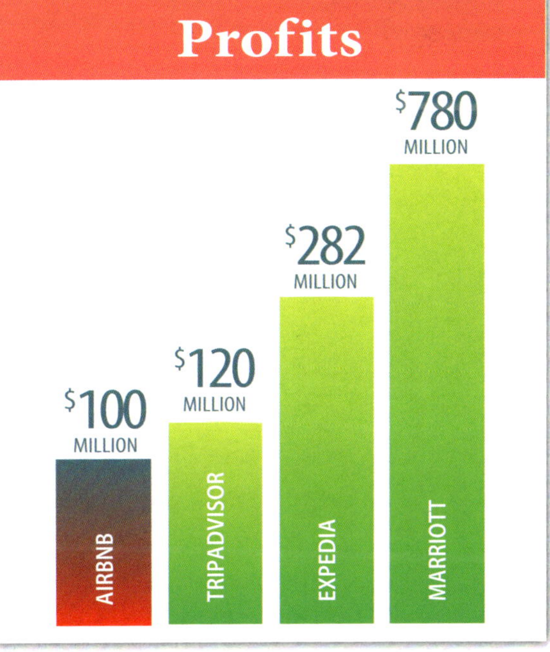

2016 Figures

Innovation and Technology

Sophisticated Searching

Airbnb's website is designed to make the task of searching and booking accommodations enjoyable and easy. Special **algorithms** have been established to narrow down a search for accommodations based on guest input. The properties that best match a guest's search criteria are shown first, with preference given to hosts that are known to take good care of their guests. Algorithms are also used to play matchmaker, allowing the site to make travel recommendations based on the wording of property listings, customer reviews, and searches.

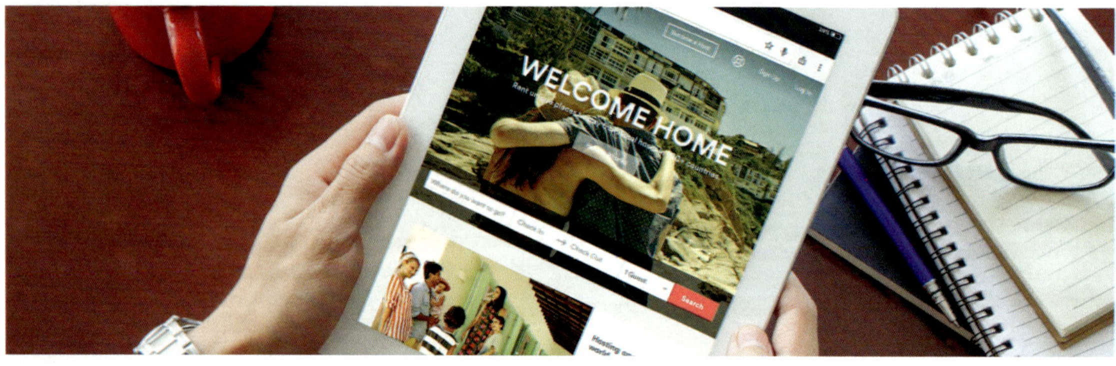

Samara

As Airbnb has shown, things change quickly for online businesses. In order to stay one step ahead of its competition, Airbnb has created its own innovation and design laboratory. Known as Samara, this facility allows Airbnb engineers, technologists, programmers, and designers to work on projects they think will help Airbnb overcome present and future challenges.

Yoshino Cedar House

The first project developed by the Samara team was the Yoshino Cedar House. Located in the Japanese village of Yoshino, the house was designed to promote relationships between its guests and the local community. Yoshino Cedar House was built by local artisans using cedar wood from nearby forests. The villagers maintain and manage the house as an Airbnb property available for rent. The house attracts visitors to the area and provides income for the community. In this way, Yoshino Cedar House helps form new relationships while also supporting the community.

Security

Airbnb has taken many steps to ensure the safety of both its hosts and guests. When a guest inquires about a property through Airbnb's website or app, his or her contact information is removed before the message is sent. This means that, until a booking is confirmed between the two parties, communication can only take place through the website or app. In 2017, Airbnb purchased Trooly. This company performs background checks on people, helping to find hosts and guests who are not following the rules set by Airbnb. Knowing their transactions are being monitored for **fraudulent** activity gives Airbnb users a sense of comfort and security.

Giving Back

Making donations and contributions to special causes is common practice among major corporations. As part of the sharing economy, the concept of giving back is especially important at Airbnb. The company encourages community involvement among its employees and has developed several programs designed to help those in need.

Open Homes At any given time, there are millions of people around the world in need of emergency shelter or temporary housing. Using its many properties around the world, Airbnb started a program to help. Since 2012, Open Homes has provided shelter to people displaced by natural disasters, war, and other issues. Through Open Homes, Airbnb hosts can make their properties available to people in need. Hosts can set a limit on the length of stay and are free to choose the circumstances that they wish to support.

Volunteering The philosophy of bringing people together drives all of Airbnb's initiatives. Through volunteering efforts, Airbnb and its employees are able to come together with, and give back to, their communities. Airbnb encourages its employees to spend time helping others by giving them four hours of paid time every month to volunteer in their communities. Each year, the company dedicates an entire week, called the Week for Good, to working with **non-profit organizations** in communities around the world.

Social Impact Airbnb's social impact experiences give hosts and their guests the opportunity to work with local non-profit organizations. These opportunities offer guests an immersive experience in the community they visit, while also allowing them to make a difference in that community. Social impact experiences cover a wide range of charitable and social initiatives. Guests can walk the dogs in a San Francisco animal shelter or make crafts in support of a women's group in Nairobi, Kenya. These experiences are designed to make both the guest and the community better through collaboration and understanding. All proceeds from social impact experiences go to the non-profit organization, rather than to the host or the guest.

The **2017 Airbnb Week for Good** consisted of more than **170 volunteer projects** in ***30 cities*** around the world.

Since 2012, more than **3,100 Airbnb hosts** have opened their homes to relief workers and victims of **65 disasters** around the world.

In 2016, members of the Airbnb community completed more than ***17,000 hours of volunteer service***.

Into the Future

Airbnb's future success depends on the company's ability to grow its customer base. To do so, it must pay attention to the types of services people want when they travel. Initially formed to provide people with a less expensive option for accommodations, Airbnb is now looking to extend its reach into other areas. Its goal is no longer just to give people only a bed and breakfast. The company is now looking to providing its guests with a complete travel experience.

In 2016, Airbnb launched its Trips program, which aims to enhance a guest's stay. The program is divided into three categories—experiences, places, and homes. The homes category covers Airbnb's core service of providing accommodations. Its places section provides Airbnb's guests with guidebooks, in which Airbnb hosts and other locals provide tips on what to see and do while in the area. Guests who want to explore the area in more depth can purchase tours and adventures through Trips' experiences category. Experiences can range from a simple two-hour walking tour to a multi-day adventure. In the future, Airbnb plans to expand the Trips program to include flight bookings and restaurant reservations, making the site a one-stop travel shop.

Airbnb is also looking to attract more **high-end** customers in the coming years. In 2017, it purchased Luxury Retreats International Inc., a company that specializes in providing elite rental accommodations. The purchase gave Airbnb access to more than 4,000 luxury homes around the world, each offering 24/7 **concierge** services. This purchase, along with the company's expansion into travel services, could indicate that Airbnb is preparing to become a **public company**. If this happens, people will be able to buy **shares** in the company and take part in its success.

Brian Chesky introduced Trips at the company's annual convention, Airbnb Open, in 2016.

It is believed that Airbnb bought Luxury Retreats International Inc. for about $300 million. Besides acquiring luxury properties in more than 100 countries, the purchase has also given Airbnb access to Luxury Retreats' expertise in the high-end travel market.

Careers at Airbnb

In order to serve its community, Airbnb relies on much more than just hosts and guests. Creating, building, and maintaining the Airbnb marketplace takes the combined efforts of many people. Working together from locations around the world, Airbnb employees are constantly striving to make their services better, and their corporation stronger. It takes a strong, dedicated team of professionals to bring Airbnb hosts and guests together.

CEO

$13.8 million+ per year

The CEO is usually the highest position in a company. A CEO is responsible for making important decisions for the company, especially in the areas of finance and future plans. He or she is in charge of all aspects of the business. The CEO helps the company run smoothly, guiding it in a successful direction. He or she oversees many departments within a company, ensuring that all divisions are running smoothly and are keeping their work within budget.

Data Scientist

$93,000–$170,000 per year

Data scientists analyze and interpret information. They spend their time gathering statistics and data on trends and patterns of concern to their industry. Studying this information helps them identify and solve problems. It also allows them to recognize opportunities for growth. Airbnb data scientists usually possess a combination of experience and education in their field. They must be comfortable and efficient writing code in a variety of computer languages.

Customer Experience Specialist

$35,000–$138,000 per year

Airbnb customer experience specialists are the company's front-line employees. They are often the first point of contact for Airbnb guests when they have questions or problems. It is the specialist's job to handle a customer's concerns in a calm, professional, and positive manner. This is a results-driven job, with the goal to keep the customer satisfied with Airbnb's services at all times.

Security Engineer

$152,000–$178,000 per year

Security engineers are responsible for ensuring the security of Airbnb's systems, programs, **infrastructure**, and data. Security issues can include attempted fraud against a user's credit card, threatening behavior by a host or guest, or hackers targeting Airbnb's database. The security engineering team anticipates, responds to, and minimizes these and other security threats.

Activity

Airbnb is constantly seeking new directions. Its recent purchase of Luxury Retreats demonstrates the company's commitment to widening its reach in the hospitality industry.

Imagine that Airbnb has asked you to develop a marketing campaign for its new luxury travel division. How would you approach this project? Use the questions below to come up with a plan.

1. Will your campaign target single travelers, couples, or families?

2. What will the theme of your campaign be?

3. What types of marketing materials will best suit your target audience?

4. Where will you place your marketing materials to attract the most customers?

5. Which features of Airbnb's luxury travel program will your campaign promote?

Quiz

1 How many countries are home to Airbnb properties?

2 In what city was Airbnb founded?

3 What is Airbnb called in China?

4 Which four images is the Airbnb logo meant to evoke?

5 What was the name of Airbnb's first global ad campaign?

6 Approximately how many employees does Airbnb have?

7 What is Samara?

8 Which Airbnb program provides temporary homes to displaced persons?

9 Who is the CEO of Airbnb?

10 What company did Airbnb purchase in 2017 to attract high-end customers?

Answers

1. 191 **2.** San Francisco **3.** Aibiying **4.** A person, a heart, a location pin, and the company name **5.** Views **6.** 3,000 **7.** Airbnb's design and innovation laboratory **8.** Open Homes **9.** Brian Chesky **10.** Luxury Retreats International Inc.

Key Words

algorithms: formulas for solving problems

app: a software program used on a desktop computer or mobile device

assets: valuable properties owned by a company or person

branding: characteristics that serve to identify a particular company

chief executive officer (CEO): the highest-ranking person in a company

concierge: a hospitality worker who provides personalized customer service

corporation: a company authorized to act as a single entity

entrepreneurship: the willingness to develop and manage a business

fraudulent: deliberately deceitful

high-end: the wealthiest or most expensive

incubator: an environment tailored to help companies thrive and grow

infrastructure: the basic structures needed for the operation of a business

investors: people who commit money to a project in order to gain a financial return

liabilities: a company's debts and business costs

logo: a symbol or design used to identify a specific company

market capitalization: the market value of a company's outstanding shares

market value: the amount for which something can be sold

microsites: individual web pages within a larger website

non-profit organizations: groups that conduct business for the benefit of the general public without a profit motive

profits: the monetary returns on a business undertaking after all operating expenses have been met

public company: a business whose shares can be bought by the general public

shares: units of ownership interest in a company

sharing economy: a system in which a person is able to borrow or rent assets owned by someone else

slogans: phrases used repeatedly to advertise products

start-up: a fledgling business that offers an innovative service or product

valuation: an estimation of how much something is worth

venture capital: money invested in a project that involves risk

Index

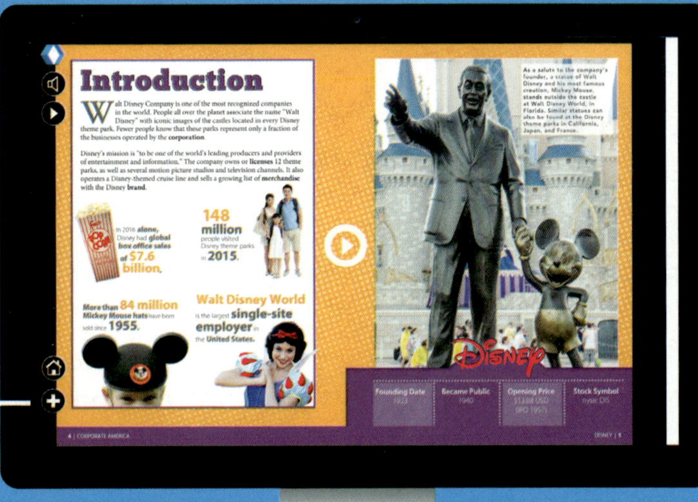

SUPPLEMENTARY RESOURCES

Click on the plus icon found in the bottom left corner of each spread to open additional teacher resources.

- Download and print the book's quizzes and activities
- Access curriculum correlations
- Explore additional web applications that enhance the Lightbox experience

LIGHTBOX DIGITAL TITLES
Packed full of integrated media

VIDEOS

INTERACTIVE MAPS

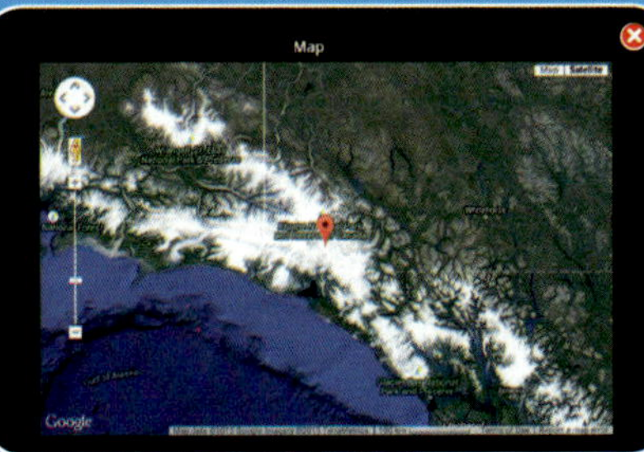

WEBLINKS

SLIDESHOWS

QUIZZES

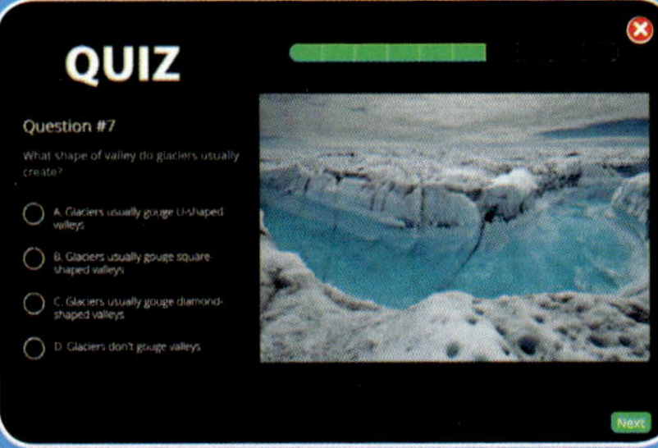

OPTIMIZED FOR

- ✔ TABLETS
- ✔ WHITEBOARDS
- ✔ COMPUTERS
- ✔ AND MUCH MORE!

Published by Smartbook Media Inc.
350 5th Avenue, 59th Floor New York, NY 10118
Website: www.openlightbox.com

Editor: Heather Kissock
Designer: Nick Newton

Library of Congress Cataloging-in-Publication Data
Names: Wiseman, Blaine, author.
Title: Airbnb / Blaine Wiseman.
Description: New York, NY : Smartbook Media Inc., [2019] |
Series: Corporate America | Includes index.
Identifiers: LCCN 2017048293 (print) | LCCN 2017048888 (ebook) | ISBN 9781510534896 (Multi-User Ebook) | ISBN 9781510534889 (hard cover : alk.paper)
Subjects: LCSH: Airbnb--Juvenile literature.
Classification: LCC TX941.A594 (ebook) | LCC TX941.A594 W57 2019 (print) | DDC 381/.142--dc23
LC record available at https://lccn.loc.gov/2017048293

Printed in Brainerd, Minnesota, United States
1 2 3 4 5 6 7 8 9 0 21 20 19 18 17

122017
151217

Photo Credits
Every reasonable effort has been made to trace ownership and to obtain permission to reprint copyright material. The publisher would be pleased to have any errors or omissions brought to its attention so that they may be corrected in subsequent printings. The publisher acknowledges Alamy, Getty Images, iStock, Shutterstock, and Newscom as its primary image suppliers for this title.